SMOKE JUMPERS
IN ACTION

BY JON WESTMARK

Published by The Child's World®
1980 Lookout Drive • Mankato, MN 56003-1705
800-599-READ • www.childsworld.com

Photographs ©: Barrett & MacKay/All Canada Photos/Glow Images, cover, 1;
Evgeny Dubinchuk/Shutterstock Images, 5; Vladimir Melnikov/Shutterstock
Images, 6; NIFC/Bureau of Land Management, 9, 12, 15; Shutterstock
Images, 10, 22; Ed Gavryush/Shutterstock Images, 16; U.S. Forest Service, 18,
28; Sky Light Pictures/Shutterstock Images, 21; Adam Springer/iStockphoto,
24; iStockphoto, 27

ISBN 9781503816329

LCCN 2016945663

Printed in the United States of America
PA02391

TABLE OF
CONTENTS

FAST FACTS

What's the Job?

- Smoke jumpers parachute into remote places to fight wildfires.

- Using mainly hand tools and chainsaws, they clear spaces of material that might burn.

- Smoke jumpers must have at least one season of wilderness firefighting experience, though most have many.

- All trainees must pass tests for strength, endurance, parachuting, tree climbing, and firefighting. All jumpers take refresher courses at the beginning of each season.

The Dangers

- Smoke jumpers risk parachuting into trees or rocky terrain.

- Fire can move in unpredictable ways, especially when the weather changes.

- When fighting fires, smoke jumpers risk being struck by burning or falling **debris**.

Important Stats

- There are fewer than 300 smoke jumpers in the United States.

- Smoke jumpers earn approximately $16 to $24 per hour and are employed four to six months per year. When fighting uncontrolled fires, they earn additional overtime and hazard pay.

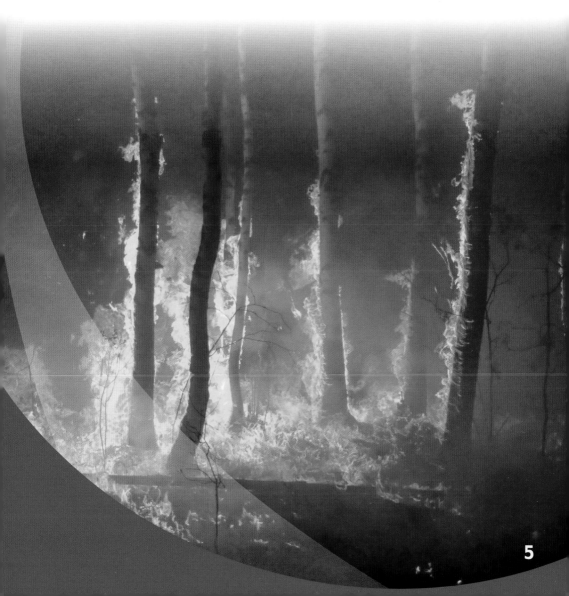

Chapter 1

HARD LANDING

Ariel Starr peered out of the open door on the side of a small airplane. The craft was circling a remote area of Alaskan wilderness near the Seventymile River. Below, flames shot up as a fire engulfed the forest.

It was late May 2015. The blaze had already burned through hundreds of acres. The fire was now threatening people's property on the opposite side of the river. There were no roads in the area. So, firefighters could not reach the fire easily by land. To protect the property, the U.S. Bureau of Land Management had called in Ariel and 15 other smoke jumpers.

Ariel had grown up in Alaska. At age 18, she had fought her first wildfire in the state. Now, she was a smoke jumper based out of Missoula, Montana. After 13 years of fighting fires, she was back in her home state on a two-month deployment.

Looking down at the river from the airplane, Ariel knew her first jump in Alaska was not going to be easy.

◀ **Smoke can make it difficult for smoke jumpers to see their landing spot.**

She and the other jumpers planned to parachute down onto a sandbar along the side of the river. The sandbar was free from trees that could snag their parachutes. But between the burning wilderness and rushing river, the jumpers had little room for error.

As the plane circled over the landing spot, the crew's **spotter** threw out streamers. Streamers show the spotter what the wind conditions are. Based on the streamers' movements, the spotter estimated the wind would push Ariel's parachute approximately 150 feet (46 m).

Ariel was not worried about the spotter's report. She was used to much windier conditions. But before the jump, the wind changed directions. Smoke from the fire rolled over the river. The sandbar became hazy and difficult to see. Despite the shift in the wind, the crew decided it was safe enough to jump.

Smoke jumpers work in pairs for safety. This way, if one person gets in trouble, the other is close by to help. Ariel and her partner were the first ones out of the plane. Both of their parachutes deployed. But as the jumpers neared the ground, the smoke made their landing spot even harder to see. Ariel decided to slow her approach so her partner could land first. As she did, the wind shifted again.

Square parachutes are designed especially for ▶ windy conditions.

Suddenly, the wind sent Ariel flying backward, away from the sandbar. She looked behind her. She was running out of dry land. If she did not touch down quickly, she would be in danger of dropping into the river. Ariel crash-landed in shallow water near the river's bank. She bent her knees and rolled against the bank to soften her landing.

The wind pushed her parachute into the water. The river's current yanked the parachute downstream, dragging Ariel with it. Ariel scraped at the dirt on the bank, trying to gain control. But the force of the current was too great. The parachute pulled her into the river.

Ariel yelled out to her jump partner. But he was too far away to help. Ariel knew she could either try to save the parachute or try to save herself. She tugged the emergency releases on her parachute harness, and she was free. Ariel made it to dry land and shed her jump helmet and padded yellow jumpsuit. The parachute floated downriver too quickly to be saved.

Ariel was not hurt from the crash landing. She and her crew spent nine days fighting the fire near Seventymile River. On the ninth day, another smoke jumper found Ariel's parachute downriver. It was torn to shreds.

◀ **Once smoke jumpers reach the ground, they use axes and other simple tools to fight fires.**

Chapter 2

CONSTANT DANGER

It seemed like an easy assignment. Lightning had struck a tree in Modoc National Forest in northeastern California. As the smoke jumpers' plane approached, light wisps of smoke floated up from a small area around the tree. Only three jumpers were needed.

Fourth-year smoke jumper Luke Sheehy was put in charge of the jump. The other two jumpers were both rookies. It was their first operation. Luke had helped train them during the intense five-week smoke jumper boot camp. Luke loved training and working with rookie jumpers. And the small, single-tree fire seemed like a perfect low-pressure situation for their first jump.

The jump went smoothly. All three men touched down in a grassy, open area. Their cargo box, too, parachuted safely to the ground. Cargo boxes contain firefighting tools and survival equipment such as food, water, and sleeping bags. The two rookie jumpers got to work unloading the box. Meanwhile, Luke radioed in a report about the scene.

◄ **A smoke jumper stands a safe distance from the fire as he waits for his supplies to land.**

The tree was a tall white pine with a crooked top. Fallen green branches smoldered in a 100-square-foot (9-sq-m) area around the tree's base. The jumpers planned to cut down the tree. Later, they would go over it inch by inch to make sure no heat lurked inside. But the heat around the tree made it impossible to reach the trunk to start cutting. Fortunately, the forest was moist. The fire was not going to spread quickly.

Luke and one of the rookie jumpers planned their attack while the third jumper assembled the chainsaw. They decided to dig a fire line around the tree. A fire line is an area in which all material that might catch fire is cleared away. The fire line is meant to stop the fire from spreading past that area. Smoke jumpers use a hand tool called a Pulaski to dig fire lines. The head of a Pulaski has an ax blade on one side and a digging tool on the other. Luke sent the rookie to begin creating the fire line.

Suddenly, there was loud crack. The crooked treetop came crashing down. One of the rookies darted out of the way just in time. The top thudded to the ground where he had been working. The treetop was on fire. It threatened to spread flames to other dead plants in the area.

A person stays inside the plane to toss supplies to the ▶ smoke jumpers.

Luke told the two rookies to create a line around the fallen treetop but to avoid going underneath the tree. After radioing in the close call, Luke joined them. Debris continued to fall from the tree. The jumpers wanted to scratch the fire line as quickly as possible. Hunched over, they worked their way around the fallen treetop.

As they were working, a large branch fell off the trunk from 60 feet (18 m) up the tree. This time, there was no loud crack. The branch quietly plummeted to the ground. By the time the rookie jumpers heard the whoosh of the falling branch, it was too late to speak up. The branch hit Luke on the head and knocked him out.

The rookie jumpers were both emergency medical technicians. They carried Luke away from the tree, tended to him, and called for an emergency helicopter. But Luke was not responding. By the time the helicopter reached a hospital, there was no chance of saving him.

Luke's death shook the tight-knit smoke jumper community. It was a reminder of the dangers even the most routine fires can pose. Approximately 1,500 people attended Luke's memorial service.

◄ **Following Luke Sheehy's death, the California state capitol flew its flags at half-staff in his honor.**

Chapter 3

MAKING A BREAK FOR IT

Jason Ramos called over the radio, but he got no response. From his command position below the fire, Jason could see the flames hurtling up the forest ridgeline. Fire as high as the treetops crackled and snapped. Moments earlier, three members of Jason's crew had been working in the area. Two had radioed that they were retreating to the safety zone at the highest point of the ridge. No one had heard from the third member of the team. Ramos called him again. No response.

It was mid-July 2013. A lightning fire had sprung up in Washington's Okanogan-Wenatchee National Forest. Jason and his crew had jumped into the area a few days earlier. But they were having trouble containing the blaze, even with the help of two helicopters dumping water on it. Jason had requested more jumpers and equipment. But none had arrived. Now, fed by 30-mile-per-hour (48-km/h) winds, the fire was growing out of control.

◄ **Okanogan-Wenatchee National Forest is in the Cascade Range, a series of mountains in the Pacific Northwest.**

Hillsides can be particularly dangerous places to fight fires. Wind can blow hot air from the fire up the slope. This air preheats the ground above the fire, allowing the ground to ignite even faster.

Jason understood how quickly hillside fires could spread. He had been in training 19 years earlier when tragedy struck firefighters on Storm King Mountain in Colorado. Jason's trainer and mentor, Rich Tyler, was one of the 49 firefighters who responded to the fire. Rich was known for his attention to safety. But when high winds caused flames to explode up the slope of the mountain, no one was prepared. The only way for the firefighters to escape the flames was to climb to the ridge. Fire chased them up the mountain. In some places, flames moved upslope at nearly 20 miles per hour (32 km/h). Rich was not able to make it to safety.

In all, 14 people died, including three smoke jumpers. Because of the tragedy at Storm King Mountain, the U.S. Forest Service made sure smoke jumpers, such as Jason, were each given a radio to improve communication.

Jason knew his crew understood the risks of their position on the hillside. All he could do was wait. Seconds later, the radio crackled to life. The third member of the team checked in.

Fire spreads much more quickly on a slope, compared to ▶ flat ground.

He had made it to the safety zone. Relieved, Jason confirmed he had received the message.

Then a wave of heat washed over Jason's face. The wind had shifted. It was now forcing the flames downhill toward the command position. Jason needed his own escape route. He called the helicopters over to his position and asked which direction looked safest from the air. One of the pilots told Jason to go up the ridge to the safety zone.

The helicopters led the way. They took turns dropping water from their buckets in front of Jason. As one helicopter dumped, the other refilled at a nearby water supply. Jason followed the helicopters' lead up the ridgeline. Flames crowded in so close he could have roasted marshmallows. After a few tense minutes of hiking, he made it to the safety zone.

The next morning, Jason returned to the fire. It had overtaken the ridge. But the extra support he requested had arrived. As the smoke jumpers walked through the burned-out area, they came across the remains of a chainsaw. One of Jason's crewmembers had dropped it the day before. The chainsaw was made of aluminum, which melts at 1,221 degrees Fahrenheit (660°C). It was now a blob of melted metal.

◄ **Chainsaws are important tools for smoke jumpers.**

Chapter 4

FIGHTING FIRE WITH FIRE

A train chugged along tracks at the base of Utah's Price Canyon. The midday sun heated the already bone-dry canyon floor. It was June 30, 2002, and Utah was in the midst of one of its worst droughts ever.

A spark from the train's locomotive was all it took. The sunbaked grass, **sagebrush**, and juniper shrubs throughout the canyon provided the fuel. Within an hour, fire had engulfed 25 acres (10 ha) of the canyon.

Smoke jumpers arrived on a **plateau** above the canyon at 5:00 p.m. The jumpers landed near a dirt road that ran alongside the canyon. The road was a perfect fire line. But if the fire from the canyon reached the road, the fire might be able to span across the street. The jumpers needed to starve the fire of as much fuel on the plateau as possible.

◄ **Utah has many canyons and unusual rock formations.**

The jumpers used flares to start a series of **backfires** along the road. These small fires would burn toward the canyon to starve the main fire of fuel. By 6:30 p.m., the jumper in charge, Shannon Orr, feared the fire might escape the canyon to the west. The blaze had already spread to an area between 300 and 500 acres (121 and 202 ha). Shannon told jumper Matt Loe to start lighting backfires along the road to the west. But after only 15 minutes, Matt returned. He had run out of flares.

By 7:00 p.m., a thick, black smoke column rose out of the canyon to the west. It was what Matt had feared. Fire spewed over the edge of the canyon. A quarter mile (.4 km) of unburned fuel sat between the flames and the jumpers.

Within seconds, the column of fire and smoke collapsed. Instead of floating upward, the heavy black smoke was pushed onto the jumpers. **Embers** the size of softballs rained down on the crew.

The crewmembers ran for their lives. Matt and jumper Tom Dwyer ran east. They believed staying in the burned-out area would protect them from flames. The smoke followed them. After 60 feet (18 m), Tom fell to his knees, unable to catch a breath of clean air. Matt stopped as well. They used hand tools to scrape away the burned and burning sagebrush underneath them.

▲ **Smoke jumpers sometimes use flares to create backfires.**

They then took out their fire shelters. A fire shelter is a lightweight, heat-resistant tent. It is a **wildland** firefighter's last line of defense. Matt and Tom pulled their metallic shelters over their bodies and went to the ground.

Meanwhile, Shannon and the other jumpers ran north. Embers fell on the unburned terrain around them. But soon the jumpers were out of the smoke column and safely on a paved road.

▲ Smoke jumpers practice their skills on obstacle courses.

Like turtles under their shells, Matt and Tom kneeled underneath their fire shelters. At times, the wind died down and they stood up, holding the shelters above them. Flames whirled beyond the burned area where the men stood. When they felt a blast of heat coming, the jumpers lay flat on the ground.

At 7:30 p.m., Tom left his shelter. He found the crew's gear nearby. Much of it had caught fire despite being in the burned-out area. After regrouping and meeting up with other fire crews, Tom, Matt, Shannon, and the other jumpers went back to work. They had risked their lives, but their job was not yet complete. They worked on the Price Canyon fire until midnight. In all, the train's spark went on to burn approximately 3,200 acres (1,295 ha) before it was put out.

THINK ABOUT IT

- Fire is sometimes good for forests. It helps get rid of dead material and makes way for new growth. How do you think fire managers decide when to stop a fire and when to let it burn?
- Because there are so few smoke jumpers, they often have to create their own equipment. Most jumpers are excellent menders. What other parts of a smoke jumper's job surprised you?
- Smoke jumpers face many different risks. Why do you think smoke jumpers and other firefighters are willing to take such big risks for their jobs?

GLOSSARY

backfires (BAK-fires): Backfires are fires set along a fire line that burn toward the main fire. Backfires starve forest fires of fuel.

debris (duh-BREE): Debris is the pieces of something that has been broken or destroyed. Debris falling from trees can be dangerous for smoke jumpers.

embers (EM-burz): Embers are the hot, glowing pieces of wood or other material in a fire. Wind moves a fire's embers through the air.

plateau (pla-TOH): A plateau is a flat area of ground that is higher than the surrounding area. Smoke jumpers often land on a plateau above a canyon.

sagebrush (SAYJ-brush): Sagebrush is a common shrub in the western United States. The Price Canyon fire quickly spread through sagebrush.

spotter (SPAHT-uhr): A spotter is a person who decides when it is safe to jump and makes sure smoke jumpers get out of the airplane safely. The spotter sometimes uses streamers to check wind conditions.

wildland (WILD-land): Wildland is land that is not managed or controlled by humans. Smoke jumpers are one type of wildland firefighter.

TO LEARN MORE

Books

Goldish, Meish. *Hotshots*. New York: Bearport, 2014.

Mara, Wil. *Smokejumper*. Ann Arbor, MI: Cherry Lake, 2015.

Reeves, Diane Lindsey. *Scary Jobs*. New York: Ferguson, 2009.

Web Sites

Visit our Web site for links about smoke jumpers: childsworld.com/links

Note to Parents, Teachers, and Librarians: We routinely verify our Web links to make sure they are safe and active sites. So encourage your readers to check them out!

SELECTED BIBLIOGRAPHY

"Price Canyon Fire Entrapment Investigation Report." *Wildland Fire Lessons Learned Center*. USDA Forest Service, 30 June 2002. Web. 11 Apr. 2016.

Ramos, Jason A. *Smokejumper: A Memoir by One of America's Most Select Airborne Firefighters*. New York: William Morrow, 2015. Print.

Starr, Ariel. "Alaskan River Landing." *The Smokey Generation*. The Smokey Generation, 2015. Web. 11 Apr. 2016.

INDEX

ABOUT THE AUTHOR

Jon Westmark is a writer and editor living in Minneapolis, Minnesota. Though he lives in the city, he is thankful for wildland firefighters, such as his sister, who help keep our wilderness healthy.